Brilliant

CW01431602

Poems by Betti Moretti
1970-2023

Worcestershire
Poet Laureate
2018-2019

Brilliant Betti

Betti Moretti
Edited by Black Pear Press

First published 2024 by Black Pear Press
www.blackpear.net
Copyright © Betti Moretti
All rights reserved.

ISBN 978-1-916910-13-3

Cover Photograph by Catherine Crosswell
Design by Black Pear Press

Black Pear Press

Have a whale of a time.....

Marie, Betti's mother, says, 'Many thanks to Betti's friend Jacky Taylor Griffin for all her hard work in helping with this poetry book. Such a support in our loss.' Worcestershire LitFest & Fringe, and Black Pear Press also extend thanks to Jacky, her input has been invaluable.

Preface

Poem written by Betti for her funeral

Let it not be said, when I am quite dead
that I never made anyone smile,
and don't worry now, with a crease in your brow
because I'm having more fun—by a mile
I'm dancing with leaves, swirling up through the air
and I'm sunlight and moonbeams, I have not a care
as I tinkle in streams and I gurgle in brooks,
wait dusty on shelves there with all the great books,
I am happy and joyous and most of all, free,
I am really and truthfully, more than me.

About Betti Moretti, Poet, Singer, Actor, Artist and Illustrator

BA (Hons) Design For Communication Media, Manchester Metropolitan University

Art & Design Foundation Course, Bournville College Of Art

Traditional Animation Course, Lighthouse, Wolverhampton

Betti introduced herself on Facebook in this way:

> 'Following a 10 year stint in film & television with written, produced & directed credits after which I was "killed off" in BBC 1's Doctors (I'm a rubbish actress), I'm now a self-employed artist and share an art studio at Bewdley Museum, Worcestershire, where I create…stuff & things and generally get up to mischief where at all possible.
>
> If you would like to see me performing a couple of poems then please go to my YouTube page at:
>
> http://www.youtube.com/user/BettiMoretti123/videos'

Elizabeth 'Betti' Moretti was a much-loved singer, actor, artist and illustrator who died aged 53 on September 30, 2023.

She was known as Lizzie to her friends but used the name Betti for her artistic work. Born in St Albans, Betti moved to Clent at three years of age and then to Belbroughton. She attended Hagley Primary School and Haybridge School in Hagley before studying at Bourneville Art College and Manchester Metropolitan University.

Betti called Bewdley home and spent the last ten years of her life in the town. She met her partner, Simon, there, though their first meeting was at middle school.

Her career in film started out alongside Richard Patching in Hagley. Her love of the arts led to Taiwan to help make a film about the apprentice of the year. She later worked on children's programmes like Scratchy and Co before becoming a production assistant at Pebble Mill Studios. More recently, she was production assistant on 'Off Grid' an acclaimed film made in Bewdley by a local director, Carl Timms, and starring Alison Steadman and James Cosmo.

Betti loved travel and adventure and took off for Thailand, coming back pregnant with her only child, Coco. She always said that her daughter Coco was her 'greatest ever achievement'.

Betti loved community events and made animals including a bear for the Wild in Art town and city trails and a statue for Zandra Rhodes' Gratitude project in support of the NHS. Betti's work raised many thousands of pounds for charity. So loved was her Bear that it was brought back to Bewdley with support from the many residents who contributed to the winning auction bid.

Betti's artistic talents were wide ranging, including music as well as art. She even formed a successful ABBA tribute band with Simon and two of her close friends.

Betti was also a talented poet as you will see in this posthumous collection celebrating her time as Worcestershire Poet Laureate 2018-2019.

Betti Moretti, Artist

Bewdley Bear–Big Sleuth in Birmingham–Wild in Art / © Daniel Graves

From Worcestershire LitFest and Fringe

At the time of writing this tribute—September 2024, we have 'anointed' 14 Worcestershire Poets Laureate, all of them unique, each one different and without exception fine poets and storytellers. We work with many of them to this day, but sadly we cannot work again with one of the most gifted and creative Laureates, 'Our Betti' who was honoured during 2018/2019. She was, quite simply, 'Brilliant Betti' and that is an apt title for this anthology of her collected works. Betti was a poet, an actor, a singer, an artist and an illustrator, a beloved daughter, partner and mum to the wonderful Coco, (who Betti brought to many events and gigs during her Laureateship). After the tenure finishes our former Laureates are ALWAYS Laureates and Betti will remain as that for all time.

She was a talented, shining star who lit up a room, a venue, a crowd or a few people. She owned every event she graced, not showily, or with bombast or ego but with a warmth, a charm and a cheeky laugh. She won hearts and minds and we were proud to know her and work with her, sadly not for long enough and that is a matter of great regret to us all. We didn't realise we had her only on loan but what a great loan she was! We hope Betti is out there somewhere, still making people laugh and cry, (usually at the same time)!

We will forever keep Betti in our hearts with deep regard and respect.

She was our Betti, a marvellous Worcestershire Poet Laureate and an extraordinary artist.
Shine on, Brilliant Betti Moretti!

Martin Driscoll, Nina Lewis and Dr Mark Robbins
Directors of the Worcestershire Literary Festival & Fringe CIC—aka LitFest

Contents

Unless otherwise stated, images are from Betti's estate. Sincere thanks to Simon Baylis, Colin Hill, Holly, Tim Finch, Daniel Graves, Robert Malby, David Oates, St Richard's Hospice, Stuart Wallace, and Rosie Walsh of Wild in Art for their support and assistance with acknowledged photographs.

© Worcester's Big Parade / St Richard's Hospice

To Whom it May Concern

My skin has turned from pale to brown,
a new fringe hides that hideous frown;
my nails are painted; I have a new dress;
I'm eating much better and I weigh a bit less.
I'm off on a journey, adventure—a quest
'cos that's what I'm good at—it's what I do best.
So, be gone docile doormat, grab life by the balls,
I'll scribble my feelings and paint them on walls,
do what I love to make myself heard,
try and get published—or is that absurd?
In betwixt shopping and cleaning etcetera
I write up my publishers' grovelling letter.
'Oh please won't you give this poor mum a fair shot?
—a crack at the whip—I'm not asking a lot.
Just a chance to be published, admired and adored
Lest the bills don't get paid whilst I die at home, bored.'

Tolkien on the Table

I ponder future echoes as I look about our house,
hoping for ideas to come and fill my head with nous.
And as I do I realise I needn't try too hard—
there's everything from history to new and avant-garde.
There's Tolkien on the table, Dr Seuss is on the stair,
Guess How Much I Love You looks inviting on the chair.
Masquerade seductively peeps out from on the shelf,
stirring up fond feelings from my young detective self.
Matilda waltzes naughtily and peeps out from the rug,
the caterpillar's starving and the giant needs a hug.
Heidi catches sunbeams from within the secret garden,
alongside Stig and Kes—and Billy Bunter begs your pardon.
The rabbit's feeling velveteen, the mouse mad as The Hatter,
The Cheshire Cat is grinning at the antics of the latter.
Robinson and Friday teach some words to pretty Poll,
as Pugwash battles pirates and Iofur Raknison hugs a doll.
Lyra's Pantalaimon changes swiftly to a bird
and swoops with Ransome's swallows sharing stories they have heard
of mountains—one's called Hushabye and gently in the breeze
Moomintroll drifts on a cloud, ignoring Stinky's tease.
Gromit swings upon a star, the moon is made of cheese,
Charlie's in a great glass lift, the Vicious Knids are pleased.
Jack and Jill go up the hill to wrestle with some water
and so I share adventures with my gorgeous little daughter.
Her eyes grow wide as saucers as I read *The Tinderbox*,
she forms her own opinions of *Fantastic Mr Fox*.
She falls in love with Harry, Ron and weirdly also Malfoy
and wields her wand as we two bond over magic and a schoolboy.
And I know my work is done here when I get my greatest wish
she discovers Douglas Adams on her own, and thanks the fish.
I've influenced future grandkids as my parents did before,
they too can laugh and ooh and ah and maybe write some more.
For home is where the heart is and we all love a good book—
especially on some cushions, snuggled, in a reading nook.

So read with all the children, let them travel far and wide
discovering new worlds on pages, teach them things with pride.
The world will be their oyster—it's the best thing we can do,
And maybe, if we're lucky, they'll write poems for us too.

A Napple a Day

'Please may I have a napple?' my sweet daughter said to me,
'A pink one, crisp and juicy from our lovely napple tree?'
'Why surely you mean apple?' I said, reaching for a fruit,
'The Bible says an apple caused all evil from its root.'
'Well I shall stick with napple then and eat one every day,
and when I see an apple I shall turn my head away.
May we go to Mowa Meadow now to watch the birds and bees?'
'Of course we can, my darling—we'll go anywhere you please.
But just be warned of bees and birds—they dine upon the apple.'
'In Mowa Meadow? I don't think so—there they grow the napple.'
So two girls went to Mow that day, the mother and her daughter
and ate the sweetest napples, happy, knowing what they oughta.

Hairy Legs

My daughter snuggled down beneath the sheepskin and the quilt,
I tucked her in so tenderly (ignored the crumbs she'd spilt).
She looked me in the eye and yawned, I knew the book was near,
unwittingly I picked it up and so unleashed The Fear.

The spider strolled out, nonchalant, across the duvet cover
And instantly the choice was made—
I'd be the World's Best Ever Mother!
(Words cannot describe the inner turmoil in my head—
one moment we were chillin'—then there's a beastie on the bed).

I could have screamed and jumped right up, gesticulating wildly,
but somehow, with a hidden strength, I acted rather mildly.
I scooped the fella carefully away from my little girl,
it fought against my fingers as my toes began to curl.

It was easily three inches with black hairs upon its back,
it eyed me octonarily—and then scuttled through a crack!
I swivelled fast, ignoring shooting pains that whipped my lumber,
determined not to let it ruin my girl's chance of a slumber.

My hand came down and gently cupped and caught the little critter,
my victory was certain but my sentiments were bitter—
I had NO CHOICE but to take control and calmly tame the beast
—the book was slid beneath its legs and I'd secured it then at least.

With not a shake nor break I smoothly raised it to my eyes—
(I couldn't help but think I was avenging all those flies).
I nudged the curtain sideways, glad the window was ajar
and out he went 'goodbye dear friend, we'll watch you from afar'

I straightened up and turned to look upon my rescued daughter
to find that she observed me, smiling, sipping from her water.
'I thought that you were going to freak and scare me half to death,

That spider was enormous—I could almost smell its breath…'

Now, a testament to both of us is surely needed here,
for in that moment neither of us showed the signs of fear.
I lay down then beside her and we both collapsed in giggles,
disaster was averted but we both had little niggles.

We could have been so frightened but we both chose to be brave
'I'll sleep with you tonight though, Mum—that was just too close a
shave.'
The bed may never be the same, it's etched upon our memory—
the night we chose to beat the fright—and of a spider, now named
Henry.

Oh the Horror!

I just had to wrestle this fella,
He was feisty and big as my hand.
I put him outside through the window,
And waited to see where he'd land.

I think he went round to the neighbours,
After falling the height of two floors,
And I say that because in the distance,
I heard screams and a couple of roars.

From Chimp in Lincoln Imp Trail

Said Imp to Chimp:
'How come you're always happy every day?'
And Chimp replied:
    'Why fruit of course—it keeps the blues away!
    Bananas, orange, mango, pear—I buy them at the shops'
'Oh no you don't!' replied the Imp, 'you fiendish cheeky-chops!
You find it in the jungle, maybe lying on the floor.'
    'Perhaps,' said Chimp, but Lincoln sells it in its local store.'
'Well I shall go and get some then,' the Imp said with a grin
and scampered off as Chimp put all his rubbish in the bin…

Genetic Wealth

Now, we've all got our fair share of problems
not to mention a great deal of woes,
but you would not believe the state of a sleeve
when my daughter blows on her nose.

Oh I ask her not to do it
and instead simply reach for a tissue,
but at eight and a bit, a dribble of spit
and some bogies is just not the issue.

There's no point in my getting all angry
or screeching until I go red,
'cos it just doesn't work, is returned with a smirk
and so I'm using bribery instead.

'I'll PAY you to clean up your bedroom
and remove all those toys from the floor—
scrub off the mould and it might be in gold
there's a big bit just there by the door.

There's a pound if you sort out the floordrobe
and please, put those books on the shelf.
Oh! Good golly! A lolly! It's welded to Dolly—
pass the scissors—I'll do that one myself.

I don't wanna step over wrappers
or deal with those stains on the floor,
there's graffiti on walls, I've trod on two balls
and at this rate I'm going to be poor.

As she looks at me, blank-faced, so lovely,
I suddenly feel myself smile
'cos it's plain to see that she's my mini-me
and I'd forgotten that fact for a while.

You see, she's PLAYED with those toys in the bedroom,
given names, made up songs, written books,
and whatever that mould was beforehand,
she probably helped me to cook.

The floordrobe's not born out of fashion—
more the desire to be someone unique,
and the books she's devoured, poured over for hours
have inspired and delighted for weeks.

Dolly's been tenderly cared for—
invited to tea and told jokes,
and with scissors quite sharp she's created great art
and I couldn't care less if I'm broke.

Each sweet was an oral explosion,
picked carefully out at the shop
and the graffiti is neat, and it's ever so sweet
with 'I love you,' in pink, at the top.

You see I'm wealthy in terms of what matters—
so rich I could burst at the seams,
and the joy that I get from my urchin
way surpasses my lottery dreams.

So we tidy the bedroom together,
and I'm ever so glad that we did—
because there, lurking, under the doll's house
I found a couple of quid.

© Tim Finch

The Offering

'But why do they do it though, mummy?' asked my daughter,
   determined to know.
So I breathed in quite deeply and offered quite weakly, 'Well, it's a
   sign that they love us—you know?'
'A sign that they love us? You're kidding! There's a kidney right
   there on the mat,
There's a mouse on the stair, a clump of red hair and the tail of
   what looks like a rat!
I don't think they love us that deeply—there's intestines and
   whiskers—a beak,
And I've never seen so many feathers!' she exclaimed as she
   crouched down to peek.
And what followed next was amazing (it's like living with
   Hermione Granger)
As the long list of entrails and organs, bowels and guts, gore and
   bones just got stranger.
'OK! You can stop now! I get it!' I exclaimed trying hard to
   distract.
'This Biology lesson is over—did I tell you we're moving? I've
   signed the new contract.'
And for a moment I thought that I'd nailed it—she sprung up with
   a beam on her face,
'Ooh! Where is it? Can we go now? Is it funky? Are there creatures
   for our cats to chase?'
And I quailed as it suddenly hit me—oh my God! What on earth
   had I done?
'Yes, dear, it's just within Bewdley—next to a safari park, second to
   none'.
Now, our kitten's the size of a Great Dane with four more year's
   growing to do
and as he expands I'd just offered him lands to explore on—right
   next to a zoo.
There's three lakes (and one's got a hippo), some rhinos, bear,
   zebra, giraffe…

and as our eyes met round a carcass, the pair of us started to laugh.
Now, I hope you don't think we're bad people—'cos in fact it is
   quite the reverse—
we're both of us lovers of nature, though our humour is sometimes
   perverse.
So we weighed up all possible outcomes—penned the words for an
   ostrich's wake,
we tripped over deer, found a buffalo's ear and woke up to a bed
   full of snakes…
and we've been in the new place three weeks now, glad the killing
   spree seems to have ceased,
and we cross twenty toes, sixteen fingers, and give praise for no
   moveable feasts.
Our cats even came with us walking—the elephants wanted to play,
but thankfully one whiff of urine and their dung sent them pelting
   away.
So all's quiet on our Worcestershire front now, anatomy lessons
   have stopped,
in fact zoology's quite taken over, and the subject of gizzards has
   been dropped.
And although our own felines are quieter, they seem happy and
   stay close to home,
there's no sign of a reindeer's antler, not a hoof, not a haunch, not
   a bone.
'But d'you think they still love us though, mummy?' whispered
   Coco this morning in bed,
'Oh I know so,' I yawned and then looked up, as the Maine Coon
   slumped down on my head.

Ode to the Trees

Now, I don't know much about trees,
but I do know that they don't have knees
I'm certain they do not grow toe-nails,
though their roots do look somewhat like entrails…
I'm sure that they like drinking water
but then again—so does my daughter
and I do know that they make me smile
and forget all my woes for a while
as they stand there—great makers of air
in the same breeze that ruffles my hair
so though they're not expert at cooking
they are certainly very good looking
and how clever that they can grow fruit!
Yes, they're brilliant from leaf-tip to root
so Hurray! for the trees with no knees
let them grow where they jolly well please
for where would we be without these guys
to lift up our chins towards blue skies?
and who cares if this rhyme sounds quite bonkers—
I'm off now to marvel at conkers
but I leave you with this little thought—
do we give trees respect as we ought?
Because really and truly without 'em
we'd be quite dead—ad infinitum…

Utter Nonsense…Ideas

Utter nonsense, blurt it out
say it, sing it, shout about
the silly, bonkers world of words,
dragons, sheep or bees and birds
in and out and up he goes
maggots dripping from his nose
frogs for breakfast, bats for tea
don't think about it carefully.
Let words fall out upon your page
and free you from your worldly cage,
make 'em big or make 'em small
invent some that make no sense at all,
ripple, ropple, rom and roo,
can't you see what words can do?
Inside, outside, up and down
the mouse king wears a little crown;
critters grin from ear to ear
cats like gin whilst dogs drink beer.
Hoople-headed, trees with hair
words can take you anywhere.
I like biscuits—you might too
let's munch them, dunk them in our stew
ants in pants and peas with pears
monkeys tumble up the stairs.

DESIGN: HAPPY HOPPY HIPPIE

ARTIST: BETTI MORETTI, ARTIST

Thirteen. . .

Now, poor old thirteen gets some terrible press
so let's make some headway and sort out this mess.
What is it with all of this mad superstition
ignored and skipped over in my maths tuition?
A three with a one (or a one with a three)
just what has thirteen ever done wrong to me?
Well—nothing! That's what! Not a thing nor a jot
and truly, I'm no mathematical swot.
It hasn't upset me or called me by names,
or indeed caused me bad luck as everyone claims.
I can't dance with it, flirt with it, take it to bed
and so needless to say it can't mess with my head!
I can't prod it or poke it or ask it to tea
'cos it's simply two numbers—THAT one and THAT three.
So what I'd like to know, and what I'd like to hear
is how come thirteen holds YOU in such fear?
Has it soaked you, provoked you or eaten your shoe?
Held you to ransom or threatened to sue?
Has it sacked you or whacked you, insulted your ears,
berated, humiliated you in front of your peers?
No?
Well then stop it I tell you! Let go of your fears!
Or poor old thirteen will be cursed for more years.
What a shame this odd number (and one that is prime)
is badmouthed and accused of such a terrible crime.
And so I say it's INNOCENT! Just let it be free…
'cos it is after all, just a one, with a three…

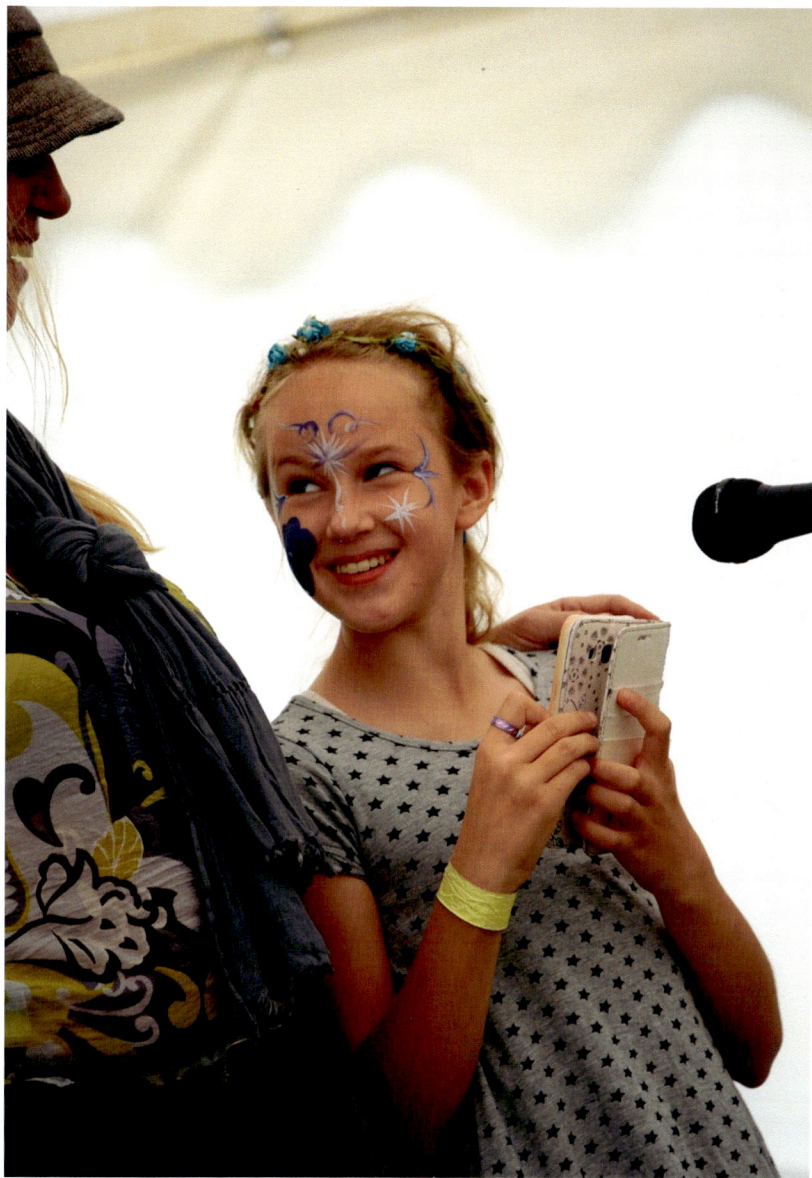

Betti with Coco © *Colin Hill*

I Want to Live upon the Sea

I want to live upon the sea
and watch the gulls fly over me,
count the fish who swim below,
befriend the stars at night aglow.
I want to live upon the sea
where no one else can bother me.

One Genius—Waiting to Happen...

Busy mum Lizzie is anything but
she has to get out of this marvellous rut.
With nothing to do but the housework it seems
that she secretly harbours some fantastic dreams...
She's an artist, a singer, a woman of wealth
she's ditched all the things that are bad for her health.
She's a painter, a writer and even a poet
she's content with herself and boy does she show it.
As the washing up mounts and the clothes lie in piles
she takes a deep breath and then grimly she smiles
for today is the day and tonight is the night
that dreams can come true and make everything right.
A plan must be planned a decision be made
(she ponders it over her pink lemonade).
She wonders how forty years flew by so fast
as she drinks to the future, won't dwell on the past.
And so out with you demons and fears and self-doubt
life's for the living, good fortune's about.
It's there for the taking, it's smiling so sweet
so get up off your chair and jump up to your feet
and then Shout! Let it out! Scream from highest of hills...
just never stop taking those wonderful pills.

Wild in Art / © Stuart Wallace

Moonlight

Moonlight shining through
glistening and dancing
brings me thoughts of you.

Light shining through my window
flooding into this empty space.
My mind filling up with thoughts of you,
as tears roll down my face.

Moonlight shining through my window,
are you seeing the same as me?
Are you seeing what I can see?
Why, oh why, can't you be here,
be here with me?

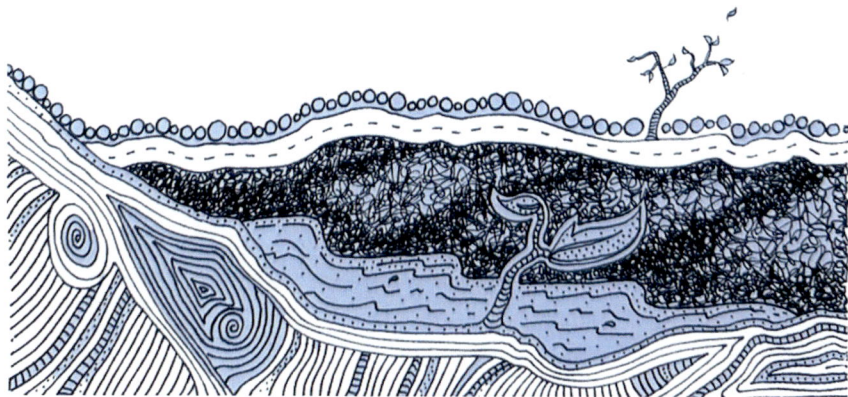

Back to Front

I love you
but know this
when you're distant
it's hard for me.
I sit by and wait
heart sinking in fear
when you return
who will you be?
Will you smile
as you walk through the door?
Will you still like me?
I know I'm not perfect
my mood's mostly steady but
when you retreat
I lose a little respect.
I don't know what you expect because
I can't just forget and
pretend it didn't happen
I just can't.
It wounds me you see, deeply,
it breaks me a little
each time I'm affected
when a kiss is deflected.

Now read from bottom to top…

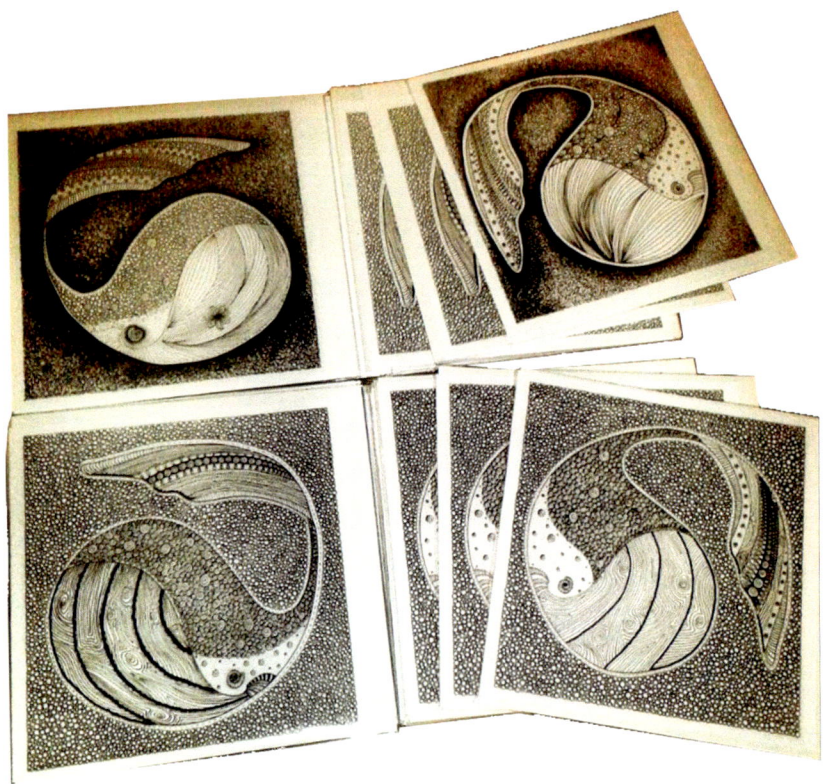

Dear Stephen…(An Openly Closed Letter)

Dear Mr Fry, just how and why do doctors miss bi-polar?
Psychos dish out Sertraline, the result? A roller coaster.
A friend of mine's in need of help—she's good and kind and stunning
but needs a hand to help her stand docs hide their heads, flee, running.
She needs the meds to clear her head, depression's not the issue,
it won't be fixed by antis mixed with sleeping tabs and tissue.
Please help us teach the docs we reach to go and do some learning,
Lest by some folly my friend Holly's deprived of the life she's yearning.
She really is a lovely girl, a single mum of three,
a shining light of humour, strength and inspiration to me.
I fight my demons earnestly—right now I am the winner,
I've ditched the pills, I'm beating ills and certainly I'm slimmer.
But I am not the issue here—I'm scrabbling for words,
My friend needs you, much-loved guru to help her needs be heard.
I'm hoping you will read this plea and spot the missing clue—
key words are what we're looking for to help her feel less blue.
Perhaps she needs to dabble with some good, old-fashioned Lithium,
Unfortunately, the pros she meets are just not bloody listenin'.
So, how to cross the huge divide—bi-polar v depression,
with doctors tired versus patients wired on another manic session.
Have you any teensy gems of knowledge you might share,
that might at least wrong-foot the beast and thus end her despair?
'Cos the reason I'm single and here all alone,
and why nobody's texting or calling my phone,
the reason I'm sitting here penning this prose
with a drink and a smoke and some sores up my nose,
the reason I ache and my eyes are all scratchy,
my muscles are twitching, my memory patchy,
the reason the house is a bit of a state,
and although I'm knackered I'll still stay up late,
and the reason I smell and my clothes all have stains…
Why! The reason is clear! It's my silly old brains!
Yours, with the utmost of faithfulness—and probably just a tad too
much vodka, Betti

Whoops-A-Daisy Foxy Lady

My hair might be quite foxy and my trousers way too tight,
but I thought I'd better make a special effort for tonight.
And I do feel kinda vulpine, but my body's in dire straits,
I was going to keep it secret but then figured well, why wait?!

I'm revelling in urine, I have lost my pelvic floor,
the weakest cough or splutter opens up my leaky door.
I'm not sure when it happened but it really is a pain,
to realise I smell as all my muscles start to wane.

I'll nip down to the chemist, just to see what I might buy,
a (crotch!) crutch to give me confidence to look you in the eye.
Oh, I'm really not embarrassed—after all it is just life,
but no wonder I'm no closer to becoming someone's wife.

I'd rather fancied Stephen Fry—could see us at our wedding
but then he wed a man instead
so I've gone with wet-look leggings.
And here I am all kneecaps trying hard to strut my stuff,
'Lay on, MacDuff, and damned be him that first cries hold!
Enough!'

It's gone WAY beyond my holding, there is nothing I can do—
except perhaps wait patiently upon the nearest loo…
but life goes on and I shall smile and hope you treat me kind,
each one of us fights hidden wars so I'm sure that you won't mind.

And later when we meet I'll curb my drinking to one half,
But listen now, and I mean it—just don't make me ruddy laugh…

sexy...?

Mirror Mirror

Today I awake in a bit of a mood
scowl at myself 'cos I hate myself nude
throw on my jim jams to lessen the pain
of seeing my ever increasing, once luxurious frame.
Mirrors! I ask you—you pain in the arse
who is the fairest—you stupid great farce
and that's when it hit me
    'You,' it replied, 'if you ever wake up without having cried.
    Your eyes are old puffy, you look like you're in pain
    Yet you still come to see me? How terribly vain
    I am a reflector, I mimic your sorrow,
    So let's have a break shall we?
    There's always tomorrow…'

Hippy Heffalump–© Robert Maltby, St Luke's Hospice Plymouth

Tributes

My Daughter

Loving thoughts of you, my dear
enduring, all my days,
great to have known you,
ever present, your little ways
never to be forgotten,
darling girl of mine.

Loved you from the beginning, your gorgeous little face
intertwining in my life
keeping me apace.
Zooming in and out,
zestful loving daughter,
inventive and creative,
entertaining with your laughter

Memories were made by you
our days were filled with fun,
remembered by your daughter Coco,
eased by you through her childhood run,
to travel on through her adult life
to know your job was done.
It's all you ever wished for, loved by everyone

Betti was your adopted name,
excelling in your art
t'would bring joy to all our hearts
to be so well remembered
on words as a poet and through your
singing too!

T'was a life well lived

for your short time.
What more could you have wished for?
A life you filled with joy and love
a life to remember.

A church mouse could not be poorer
but you faced your life with glee,
a genius waiting to happen,
happened surely for Coco and me!

Marie Moretti

Sentient Thoughts of My Daughter's Life

Your short life has unfolded
your father would be so proud,
you were your father's daughter
of that there was no doubt.
He too believed enjoying life
was what it was all about.

So, enjoy your free loving spirit,
wherever you may be,
someday I hope we'll meet again,
Coco, you and me.

Marie Moretti

Betti, her daughter Coco and mum, Marie–© Simon Baylis

Peace of Mindfulness–Wild in Art / © David Oates

A Final Word from Betti

Betti posted this to Facebook on the last day of her Laureate year:

This is it!
My last day as Worcestershire Poet Laureate…and what a
year it's been! It's been an honour…and in performing at so
many locations and events, I've come to realise how many
people gain so much from poetry—whether they be
listening, performing or writing their own.

I was particularly keen to make it fun for all—and that's
what it's been—a sometimes hilarious peek into the worlds
of others, and one I've been privileged to have been party to.

One place that particularly delighted me was Drake
Hall—a women's prison in Staffs. Eleven ladies, thirteen
poems and a pamphlet later I was blown away by their
enthusiasm and talent—a humbling experience that will stay
with me forever—not least of all because of the moment a
murderer whispered in my ear "Your flies are undone"…
😊

So, I shall keep on scribbling words and continue to try &
inspire folk to give it a go, and be forever grateful that I got
the chance, for one year, to champion poetry for the
wonderful county of Worcestershire…

I'm on the judging panel today—three very strong
finalists—and at this moment, I can't call it…who will it be,
who will the new Laureate be?!!

Anyhow, I'm jumping in the car now and wending my
merry way to Worcester so I'll sign off for now—and my
next post? Well, that'll be announcing the next
Worcestershire Poet Laureate so watch this space!

Many thanks to Worcestershire LitFest & Fringe for
having me—it's been a blast! 😃 #wpl…

© Colin Hill

Betti at a launch with Stephen Fry © Holly

Wild in Art / © *David Oates*